The Victorian Trumpet

8 Sensational Solos for trumpet and piano
8 Superbes Solos pour trompette et piano
8 Wirkungsvolle Stücke für Trompete und Klavier

Selected and arranged by John Wallace and Tony Rickard

Contents

© 2001 by Faber Music Ltd
First published in 2001 by Faber Music Ltd
3 Queen Square London WC1N 3AU
Music set by Tony Rickard
Printed in England by Caligraving Ltd

ISBN10: 0-571-52053-7
EAN13: 978-0-571-52053-4

Introduction

Brass players were the pop stars of the Victorian age; the best of them could fill a hall just by putting their names on a poster. Popular entertainment flourished and parlour songs such as these would have been heard not just in the home, but in many of the penny gaffs and music halls that dotted the towns of Victorian England.

Liberated by the newly invented valve, brass instruments abounded in promenade concerts, music halls, and outdoors in the form of Salvation Army bands, brass bands and military bands. Cornets, trumpets and flugel horns were especially popular—to which instruments this book of wonderfully characterful and infectiously attractive music is devoted. I would like to dedicate the volume to my mother, Anne Drummond Wallace.

Notes

The Trumpeter

Though *The Trumpeter* was written in 1904 during the Edwardian period, there is good justification to include the work here: proof that the music hall and ballad tradition of the Victorians lasted well into the twentieth century. This particular song, with its military gait, was a great favourite and is a gift to our instrument. Be sure to exaggerate the echo in bars four and five of the theme.

The Lost Chord

This archetypal Victorian ballad, composed in 1877 to words by Adelaide Proctor, has been arranged for every instrument under the sun. Time has not diminished its power, and a thoughtful, intense performance will still reduce many a strong man or woman to tears.

The Holy City

When a student gains the considerable stamina to bring off *The Holy City* with requisite fervour and drama, it is an indication of their growing maturity. Once prevalent in brass band solo contests, this piece has dropped from view recently. Here it is reinstated as a serving of musical greens—good for your lung-power, lip, and also for your soul!

'Sorry her lot who loves too well'
from *H.M.S. Pinafore*

In Gilbert and Sullivan's operetta, *H.M.S. Pinafore*, 'Sorry her lot who loves too well' is the ballad that introduces Josephine, the captain's daughter. The trumpet and cornet have been dab hands at melancholy ever since the second movement of the Haydn Trumpet Concerto, and this particular ballad strays into an area of even greater strength—sentimentality.

The Last Rose of Summer

Irish songs were all the rage during the Victorian and Edwardian periods. This tender and wistful love song, which comes from the same stable as the *Londonderry Air*, needs delicate treatment from the player. Use it to work at your control of soft dynamics, production and sound.

The Posthorn Galop

Koenig was a phenomenally successful cornet soloist in the first half of the nineteenth century, and toured the world with the orchestra of Jullien, the greatest musical showman of the age. His *Posthorn Galop* is one of a handful of pieces from this period to have remained in the popular repertoire of the trumpeter. It makes a great encore or finish to any concert: use a short posthorn in A flat if available, and play at breakneck speed!

The Ash Grove

Traditionally the first air that a young player, brought up in the brass band system of transmitting playing skills aurally, would perform after mastering a long slow melody like *The Holy City*. Victorian brass soloists were spectacularly virtuosic and this is the sort of solo they would have cut their teeth on. Two schools of thought exist regarding the variations: 1) strict tempo throughout; 2) make each one as different as possible. See which you prefer!

Bill Bailey, won't you please come home?

The America of this period had its own forms of music hall called 'Vaudeville' and 'Burlesque'. By the 1890s the 'Tin Pan Alley' publishing movement, which churned out popular songs, was already in full flow. American acts—especially minstrel shows—took the world by storm. The syncopated tune of *Bill Bailey* takes its cue from ragtime and is an early pointer towards jazz.

John Wallace

To buy Faber Music publications or to find out about the full range of titles available please contact your local music retailer or Faber Music sales enquiries: Faber Music Limited, Burnt Mill, Elizabeth Way, Harlow, CM20 2HX England Tel: +44 (0) 1279 82 89 82   Fax: +44 (0) 1279 82 89 83 sales@fabermusic.com   www.fabermusic.com

Avant-propos

Les cuivres furent les «pop stars» de l'ère victorienne; les meilleurs d'entre eux pouvaient remplir une salle sur la seule foi de leur nom apposé sur une affiche. Les divertissements populaires fleurissaient et les chansons de salon, comme celles proposées ici, résonnaient dans les maisons, mais aussi dans nombre des beuglants et des music-halls qui émaillaient les villes de l'Angleterre victorienne.

Libérés par l'invention récente du piston, les cuivres abondaient dans les concerts-promenades, les music-halls et, en plein air, dans les fanfares de l'Armée du salut, les orchestres de cuivres et les musiques militaires. Les cornets à pistons, les trompettes et les bugles à pistons étaient particulièrement populaires—instruments auxquels ce recueil de pièces merveilleusement pittoresques, à la séduction contagieuse, est consacré. Je souhaiterais dédier ce volume à ma mère, Anne Drummond Wallace.

Remarques interprétatives

The Trumpeter

Bien qu'écrit en 1904, durant la période édouardienne, *The Trumpeter* ne départ en rien dans ce recueil: il est la preuve que le music-hall et la tradition des ballades des Victoriens perdurèrent au XXe siècle. Ce chant particulier, aux allures militaires, fut un grand succès et est un don pour notre instrument. Assurez-vous d'exagérer l'écho dans les mesures quatre et cinq du thème.

The Lost Chord

Cette ballade, archétype de l'ère victorienne, composée en 1877 sur des paroles d'Adelaide Proctor, a été arrangée pour tous les instruments possibles. Le temps n'a en rien amoindri son pouvoir, et une interprétation réfléchie, intense fera encore venir les larmes à plus d'un auditeur robuste.

The Holy City

Lorsqu'un étudiant acquiert l'endurance considérable indispensable à l'exécution de *The Holy City* avec la ferveur et le drame requis, c'est le signe de sa maturité grandissante. Naguère répandue dans les compétitions solistes d'orchestres de cuivres, cette pièce est récemment tombée dans l'oubli. Nous vous réservons ici ce plat de légumes verts musicaux—bon pour votre capacité pulmonaire, vos lèvres, mais aussi votre âme!

«Sorry her lot who loves too well»
from *H.M.S. Pinafore*

Dans l'opérette de Gilbert et Sullivan, *H.M.S. Pinafore*, «Sorry her lot who loves too well» est la ballade qui introduit Josephine, la fille du capitaine. La trompette et le cornet à pistons ont toujours été doués pour la mélancolie, depuis le deuxième mouvement du Concerto pour trompette de Haydn, et cette ballade particulière erre dans une région d'une force plus grande encore—la sentimentalité.

The Last Rose of Summer

Les mélodies irlandaises firent fureur aux époques victorienne et édouardienne. Cette chanson d'amour, tendre et mélancolique, dans la veine du *Londonderry Air*, requiert un traitement délicat de la part de l'interprète. Servez-vous en pour travailler votre maîtrise des dynamiques douces, votre émission et votre sonorité.

The Posthorn Galop

Koenig fut un joueur de cornet à pistons qui connut un succès phénoménal dans la première moitié du XIXe siècle—il fit le tour du monde avec l'orchestre de Jullien, le plus grand showman musicien de son temps. Son *Posthorn Galop* est l'une des rares pièces de cette époque à être demeurée au répertoire populaire des trompettistes. Elle constitue un formidable bis ou morceau de fin de concert: utilisez, si possible, un petit cor de postillon en la bémol et jouez à tombeau ouvert!

The Ash Grove

Traditionnellement le premier air qu'un jeune interprète, éduqué dans le cadre des orchestres de cuivres, où la maîtrise du jeu est transmise oralement, exécuterait après une longue et lente mélodie comme *The Holy City*. Les cuivres victoriens solistes étaient d'une virtuosité spectaculaire et c'est là le genre de solos sur lesquels ils se faisaient les dents. Deux écoles existent quant au traitement des variations: 1) adopter un tempo strict de bout en bout; 2) rendre chacune aussi différente que possible. À vous de voir laquelle vous préférez!

Bill Bailey, won't you please come home?

À cette époque, l'Amérique avait ses propres formes de music-hall—le «vaudeville» et le «burlesque». Dans les années 1890, le mouvement éditorial de «Tin Pan Alley», qui produisait des chansons populaires à la chaîne, était déjà sur sa lancée. Les numéros américains—notamment les «minstrel shows» (NdT: spectacles de variétés donnés par des interprètes grimés en Noirs)—connaissaient un succès foudroyant dans le monde entier. La mélodie syncopée de *Bill Bailey*, inspirée du Ragtime, laisse déjà entrevoir le jazz.

John Wallace

The Trumpeter

J. Airlie Dix

The Lost Chord

Arthur Sullivan

The Holy City

Stephen Adams

The Victorian Trumpet

The Trumpeter

J. Airlie Dix

The Lost Chord

Arthur Sullivan

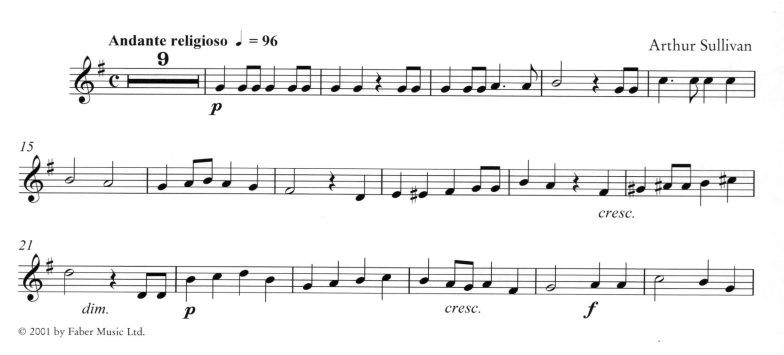

The Holy City

Stephen Adams

'Sorry her lot who loves too well'

from *H.M.S. Pinafore*

Arthur Sullivan

6

The Last Rose of Summer

Traditional Irish

Andante cantabile ♩ = 66

[music notation]

© 2001 by Faber Music Ltd.

The Posthorn Galop

Hermann Koenig

© 2001 by Faber Music Ltd.

* TRIO: *Tacet* if played on Posthorn

The Ash Grove

Traditional

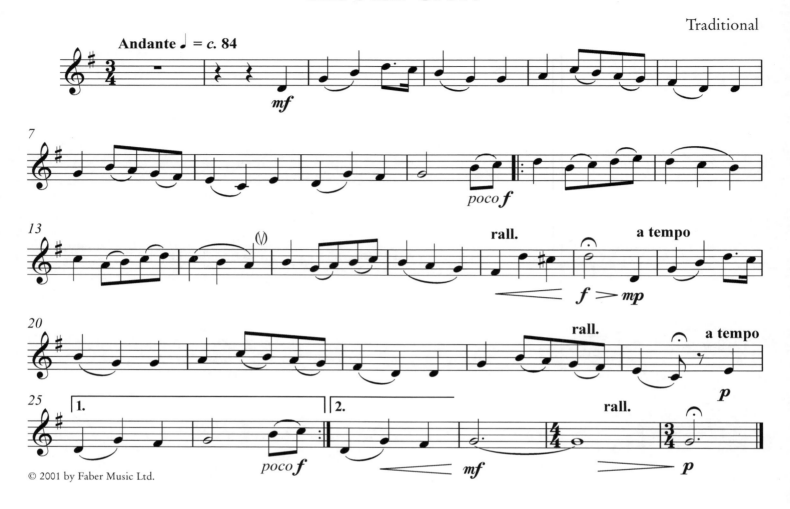

Bill Bailey, won't you please come home?

Hughie Cannon

'Sorry her lot who loves too well'

from *H.M.S. Pinafore*

Arthur Sullivan

The Last Rose of Summer

Traditional Irish

The Posthorn Galop

Hermann Koenig

* TRIO: *Tacet* if played on Posthorn.

The Ash Grove

Traditional

Bill Bailey, won't you please come home?

Hughie Cannon

Vorwort

Blechbläser waren die Popstars des viktorianischen Zeitalters. Die besten Vertreter dieses Faches füllten durch die bloße Erwähnung ihres Namens auf einem Plakat ganze Säle. Öffentliche Vergnügungslokale erfreute sich größter Beliebtheit. Lieder aus dem Salonrepertoire wie die hier abgedruckten hörte man nicht nur zu Hause, sondern in den vielen Varietés, die im England dieser Zeit in allen Städten zu finden waren.

Blechblasinstrumente in großer Zahl hörte man bei Promenadenkonzerten, in öffentlichen Tanzlokalen und bei Freiluftkonzerten von Heilsarmee, Blaskapellen und Militärkapellen. Die Möglichkeiten dieser Instrumente waren durch die Erfindung der Ventile erst kurz zuvor erheblich erweitert worden. Hörner, Trompeten und Flügelhörner waren besonders beliebt—diesen Instrumenten sei die vorliegende Sammlung außerordentlich charakteristischer und auf ansteckende Art und Weise begeisternder Musik gewidmet. Persönlich möchte ich diesen Sammlung meiner Mutter, Anne Drummond Wallace, zueignen.

Anmerkungen

The Trumpeter

Obwohl *The Trumpeter* 1904 während der Regierungszeit Zeit Edwards. VII. komponiert wurde, ist das Werk mit gutem Grund Bestandteil dieser Sammlung: als Beleg dafür, daß die viktorianische Tradition von „music hall" (Varieté) und „ballad" (volkstümliches, sentimentales Lied) weit ins 20. Jahrhundert hinüberreichte. Dieses Stück mit seinem besonderen militärischen Duktus war äußerst beliebt und bedeutet ein wahres Geschenk für unser Instrument. Bei der Interpretation sollte man keinesfalls versäumen, das Echo in den Takten vier und fünf des Themas stark zu überzeichnen.

The Lost Chord

Diese typische viktorianische Ballad, die 1877 zu einem Text von Adelaide Proctor komponiert wurde, gibt es in jeder nur denkbaren instrumentalen Bearbeitung. Mit den Jahren hat das Stück nicht an Wirkung verloren, und eine sorgfältige, spannungsreiche Aufführung vermag nach wie vor manchen im Publikum zu Tränen rühren.

The Holy City

Erlangt ein Schüler genügend Durchhaltevermögen, um *The Holy City* mit der notwendigen Überzeugungskraft und dramatischen Intensität zu interpretieren, zeugt er so von seiner zunehmenden Beherrschung des Instruments. Nachdem dieses Stück früher bei Wettbewerben für Blechbläser solo viel zu hören war, ist es in letzter Zeit ein wenig in den Hintergrund getreten. Hiermit wird es von neuem als gesunde musikalische Kost angeboten: gut für die Lunge, für die Lippenspannung, und auch für das Gemüt!

„Sorry her lot who loves too well"
from *H.M.S. Pinafore*

In Gilbert und Sullivans Operette *H.M.S. Pinafore, or The Lass that Loved a Sailor* (Ihrer Majestät Schiff „Schlabberlatz" oder Die Maid, die einen Seemann liebte) wird Josephine, die Tochter des Kapitäns mit der Ballad „Sorry her lot who loves too well" eingeführt. Trompete und Kornett haben sich seit dem zweiten Satz von Haydns Trompetenkonzert hervorragend auf die Erzeugung melancholischer Klänge verstanden; diese Ballad geht darin sogar noch ein wenig weiter, bis hin zur Sentimentalität.

The Last Rose of Summer

Irische Lieder waren zur Zeit von Queen Victoria und King Edward überaus in Mode. Dieses zarte und nachdenkliche Liebeslied, das der selben Quelle wie die *Londonderry Air* entstammt, muß sorgfältig musiziert werden. An diesem Stück läßt sich die Beherrschung leiser dynamischer Schattierungen, die Tonerzeugung im *piano* und zurückhaltender Klangfarben hervorragend üben.

The Posthorn Galop

Koenig war ein unglaublich erfolgreicher Kornettist in der ersten Hälfte des 19. Jahrhunderts. Mit dem Orchester des zu seiner Zeit bedeutendsten musikalischen Unterhaltungstalents Jullien reiste er um die Welt. Sein *Posthorn Galop* gehört zu den wenigen Stücken aus diesen Jahren, die sich im Repertoire der Trompete erhalten haben. Das Stück eignet sich hervorragend zum Abschluß eines Programms oder als Zugabe: Falls möglich, sollte man ein kurzes Posthorn in As einsetzen und in halsbrecherischem Tempo spielen.

The Ash Grove

Ein junger Blechbläser, der in der Tradition solcher Blaskapellen ausgebildet ist, in denen Spieltechnik nach dem Gehör vermittelt wird, würde nach einer langen langsamen Melodie wie *The Holy City* typischerweise als erstes diese Air musizieren. Solistische Blechbläser zur Zeit des Viktorianismus zeichneten sich durch außerordentliche Virtuosität aus, Stücke wie dieses waren Grundlage ihrer Ausbildung. Bei den Variationen gibt es zwei verschiedene Interpretationsansätze: 1) durchweg in einem Tempo, 2) jede Variation so unterschiedlich wie möglich zu interpretieren. Man entscheide hier selbst, was mehr gefällt.

Bill Bailey, won't you please come home?

In Amerika hießen zu dieser Zeit öffentliche Tanzlokale „Vaudeville" und „Burlesque". Um 1890 florierten schon die unter dem Namen „Tin Pan Alley" bekanntgewordenen Publikationen, massenhafte Veröffentlichungen populärer Lieder. Die amerikanischen Darbietungen, vor allem die Minstrel Shows, eroberten die Welt im Sturm. Die synkopierte Melodie von *Bill Bailey* hat ihre Wurzeln im Ragtime und weist schon auf den Jazz voraus.

John Wallace